CITY OF LIGHT, CITY OF DARK

A RICHARD JACKSON BOOK

CITY OF LIGHT, CITY OF DARK

A COMIC-BOOK NOVEL

story by **AVI** art by **BRIAN FLOCA**

SCHOLASTIC INC.

New York   Toronto   London   Auckland   Sydney

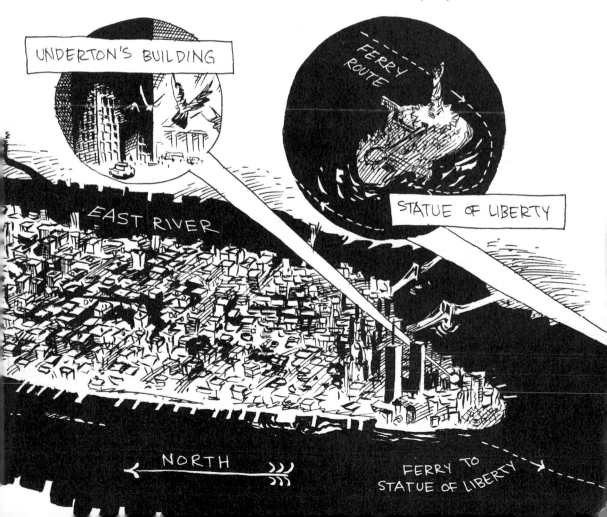

UNDERTON'S BUILDING

FERRY ROUTE

STATUE OF LIBERTY

EAST RIVER

NORTH

FERRY TO
STATUE OF LIBERTY

Text copyright © 1993 by Avi.
Illustrations copyright © 1993 by Brian Floca.
Spanish translation by José Aranda and Anthony Trujillo.
All rights reserved. Published by Scholastic Inc., 555 Broadway,
New York, NY 10012, by arrangement with Orchard Books.
Book designed by Mina Greenstein.
The text of this book is hand lettered. The illustrations are rendered
in pen and india ink applied with a brush.
Printed in the U.S.A.
ISBN 0-590-20858-6

2 3 4 5 6 7 8 9 10   2 3   01 00 99 98 97 96 95

For Shaun and Kevin

— AVI

For my parents

— B.F.

These Kurbs owned an Island as well as the sky above it. And with their POWER they controlled both day and night. For Kurbs have always thrived in darkness, turning to the dark as moths turn to light.

Years ago, when People first came to the Kurbs' Island, they wanted to build themselves a City there. First, however, they had to ask permission of the Kurbs. To this request the Kurbs' leader replied,

PEOPLE! THE LAND YOU WISH TO BUILD ON BELONGS TO US, THE KURBS. STILL, WE ARE WILLING TO LEND YOU THIS ISLAND AS WELL AS OUR POWER SO YOU MAY HAVE THE LIGHT AND WARMTH YOU HUMANS REQUIRE. BUT THERE IS A PRICE. EACH YEAR YOU MUST ENACT A RITUAL TO SHOW YOU ACKNOWLEDGE THAT THIS ISLAND REMAINS OURS AND IS GOVERNED BY OUR RULES. IF YOU FAIL TO PERFORM THIS RITUAL —BE WARNED!—THE CONSEQUENCES FOR YOU WILL BE DIRE!

To this pronouncement the People listened and finally agreed. So the Kurbs established—

The Treaty of
THE RITUAL CYCLE OF ACKNOWLEDGMENT
THAT THIS ISLAND BELONGS
TO THE KURBS

Whereas:

1) Each year, on the 21st day of June, the Kurbs shall hide their POWER somewhere in some form in the People's City.

2) The People will have six months to search for it.

3) When the People find the POWER, they shall return it to a place of safekeeping, designated by the Kurbs, no later than noon on the 21st day of December.

4) If the POWER is *not* returned, the City will grow so dark and so cold that it will *freeze*.

5) And the Kurbs will take their Island back.

Furthermore:

6) From the moment the Kurbs hide their POWER on the 21st of June, the hours of City daylight shall begin to decrease.

7) When the POWER is ritually returned to its place of safe-keeping on the 21st of December, City days shall start to grow warm. The hours of daylight will lengthen.

Finally:

8) THE RITUAL CYCLE OF ACKNOWLEDGMENT marks two halves of the human year, December to June, June to December. For the first six months the POWER shall be kept safe in a place designated by the Kurbs. For the second six months the POWER will be hidden somewhere in the city, and the People must search for it. Should the People fail to find the POWER and return it, the Cycle will be broken and the People's lease on this island shall be ended *forever*.

AGREED _____   AGREED _____
　　　　　　　For the People　　　　　　　　　　　　For the Kurbs

Signed on the 45th day of the 13th moon, Kurb year 55122337.

In the early years of this agreement the Kurbs' POWER was hidden in an ear of corn, then a musket ball. Later it was put in an oil lamp. Most recently the POWER has been put within a transit token, the small golden disk used by the People as fare for bus or subway travel.

Who searches for this POWER?

The People chose a woman. She alone had the responsibility of conducting the search. To help her in her searching, the People gave her powers that included special sight.

Now, when this woman had a daughter, the first thing she did was give that girl those powers. Only when the girl was older did her mother provide her with knowledge of the search as well as her future responsibilities. This meant that when the woman died, there was someone new to take up the yearly search. Thus, THE RITUAL CYCLE OF ACKNOWLEDGMENT continued,

mother to daughter, mother to daughter, generation after generation.

Now, the means by which the woman passed on her special powers was simple: the POWER—in whatever its form—was held to the baby's forehead. From that moment the daughter was fated to take on the searcher's responsibilities.

For hundreds of years the cycle of seeking the POWER and of returning it to the safekeeping of the Kurbs continued unbroken. Then, eleven years ago, something very different happened.

In the City there lived a man by the name of Thor Underton. He was a maker of neon signs of every imaginable color—creations brilliant enough to surpass the grandest fireworks, bright enough to turn night into day.

Underton wanted his signs large and built them so. But the larger they grew, the more costly they became to construct and electrify. Indeed, so great was their cost that people began to reject his dazzling designs.

FOOLS!

THEY CAN'T APPRECIATE GENIUS EVEN WHEN THEY SEE IT.

ALL RIGHT, THEN, I'LL MAKE THE LARGEST SIGN IN THE WORLD.

THEY'LL **HAVE** TO NOTICE ME!

Underton set to work with the assistance of his young apprentice, one Theodore Bitner.

Underton had found Theo abandoned on a dark city street. He took him in, fed and clothed him, and taught him much about sign making and electricity. Naturally, Theo wished to please Underton.

After much time and many difficulties, Underton—with Theo's help—completed his masterwork—the largest neon sign ever attempted—a gigantic spectacle of sparkling, blazing, blinking, flashing color. Its letters read,

Underton considered atomic power, solar power, sea power, wind power—nothing was enough.

Frantic, he spent hours in libraries. He consulted the Moderns. He studied the Ancients. In so doing he stumbled upon the history of the Kurbs and *their* POWER.

Further research revealed that in recent times this POWER resided in a City transit token.

But would Underton be able to find the one token from among the millions of tokens that existed? He looked for a year but did not find it.

Then he learned that, at that time, the person whose mission it was to search for the token was a young woman named Asterel. He would wait until *she* found the small golden disk. Then, *before* she could restore the token to its place of safekeeping, he would take it and thus gain control of the Kurbs' POWER!

Slyly, Underton confided in Theo about the Kurbs, the POWER, and THE RITUAL CYCLE OF ACKNOWL-EDGMENT.

Theo had no trouble meeting Asterel: he merely parked a car by a fire hydrant. She—a meter maid—gave him a parking ticket. But once the young man and young woman met, they came to like each other. What's more, in the course of time, from January to February, they fell in love.

But the more deeply Theo and Asterel loved, the greater grew their fear that the truth of their identities, if discovered, would split them apart. So they held fast to their secrets—he to the nature of his assignment from Underton, she to her fated mission as the searcher of the POWER.

In the month of March, they married.

Three months after the marriage—at the moment of noon on the 21st of June—Asterel secretly resumed that year's mission of searching for the token hidden by the Kurbs. Theo—just as secretly—spied on her, so he knew when she found the token. But he did not know why his wife slipped off to an underground hideaway beneath the City's Grand Central Station. Though he followed her there, he was unable to see her conceal the token in a hiding place of her own. The truth is, Asterel was to have a baby in December and she needed to keep the token so as to anoint the unborn child. Of that, Theo knew nothing.

In the third week of December, Asterel gave birth to a girl. "Let's name her Estella," she told Theo happily. "The word means 'star.'"

By the morning of the 21st of December, Asterel had regained enough strength to make some excuse to her husband, then slip away to her underground hideaway and fetch the token. With it she intended to anoint her daughter, passing on to Estella the searcher's gift of special sight.

Token in hand to anoint Estella, Asterel returned to the home she shared with Theo. There she found a note:

In rage and panic, Asterel raced to Underton's workshop. Instead of bargaining with the genius of light, she commenced to destroy his great sign, shattering the neon tubes into a million slivers of glass. When Underton tried to stop her and save his masterwork, he was accidentally blinded.

Now Asterel faced a terrible decision: should she complete the ritual of the token or set off to search for her baby? She felt she had no choice. She must save the city. In agony she fled the workshop, struggled through the City, and restored the token to its place of safekeeping. Then she fairly flew back to Lantern Street. But Underton, Theo, and her Estella were nowhere to be seen.

That was eleven years ago. In the time since—

Asterel has continued to do as she was meant to do—search for the token and complete the annual ritual. *But she has never stopped looking for her daughter.*

Theo has cared for Estella as lovingly as any father could. But, fearful that Asterel might find him and take their child, he has changed his name, disguised his face, and meekly given over control of his life to Underton. *Above all, he has tried to stay hidden from Asterel.*

As for Underton, he, embittered by blindness, has grown more and more obsessed about the token. Absolutely convinced that its POWER can restore his sight, he devotes all his time, energy, and genius to one goal: *that the token shall be his!*

1ST CHAPTER

THE CITY, THE AFTERNOON OF DECEMBER NINETEENTH.

THE JUAREZ FAMILY — CHILDREN, PARENTS, UNCLES, AUNTS, GRANDPARENTS, AND COUSINS — ARE ALL CHEERFULLY EXHAUSTED FROM EATING TOO MUCH. AMONG THE EXHAUSTED ONES IS CARLOS.

HE'S SITTING ALONE NEAR A SLIDING DOOR OVERLOOKING A SMALL BALCONY.

WHAT CARLOS SEES OUTSIDE UPSETS HIM.

FOR THE VIEW CONTAINS EVERYTHING HE HATES ABOUT THE CITY: IT'S BLEAK, UGLY, AND BORING.

AS CARLOS WATCHES, A SCRUFFY SPARROW FLITS THROUGH THE AIR. THE BOY SIGHS. FLYING IS THE WAY HE PLANS TO FLEE THE CITY AND GO HOME, WHERE IT'S WARM AND GREEN.

SOON... SOON.

AS CARLOS WATCHES THE SPARROW...

SAFE WITHIN THE BUILDING, CARLOS CATCHES HIS BREATH. THE BIRDS HAVE TORN HIS SHIRT. HE FEELS BLOOD ON HIS CHEEK.

WHAT MADE THOSE PIGEONS SO FEROCIOUS?

HE LOOKS AT THE DISK HE HAS TAKEN FROM THE DEAD BIRD.

WHAT'S THE BIG DEAL? JUST AN ORDINARY TOKEN.

IS THAT MAN LOOKING FOR ME?

CAN'T BE— HE'S BLIND.

IN THE BEDROOM CARLOS PUTS ON HIS JACKET TO KEEP THE TEARS IN HIS SHIRT FROM BEING SEEN, THEN TURNS UP THE COLLAR TO HIDE HIS SCRATCHES.

HOLA, MAMÁ.

"HI, MOM."

CARLOS! ME TEMO QUE TENEMOS QUE IRNOS PRONTO A CASA.

"CARLOS! I'M AFRAID WE HAVE TO GO HOME SOON."

¿PUEDO MIRAR EL FINAL DE ESTO? ES ACERCA DE LOS PRIMEROS AEROPLANOS.

POR SUPUESTO.

I'LL FLY FARTHER THAN THEY DID.

"CAN I WATCH THE END OF THIS? IT'S ABOUT EARLY AIRPLANES."

"SURE."

MEANWHILE, THE BAG LADY REACHES GRAND CENTRAL STATION....

SIGH...

34

NOW SHE IS HERSELF AGAIN—
ASTEREL, THE TOKEN SEARCHER.

WHO HAS THE TOKEN?

SHE MAKES A FIST.

IT'S THIS BOY WHO HAS IT.

ONLY THIRTY-SIX HOURS BEFORE THE DEADLINE. IF I DON'T PUT THAT TOKEN WHERE THE KURBS WANT IT, THE CITY WILL FREEZE!

FIND THE BOY! BUT THE CITY HAS MILLIONS OF BOYS. IF I DO FIND HIM, HOW WILL I GET IT FROM HIM? I'M TIRED OF BEING THE ONLY ONE DOING THIS JOB!

I WISH I COULD SEE ESTELLA.

BUT I DON'T KNOW WHAT SHE LOOKS LIKE ANYMORE AND I CAN SEE ONLY PEOPLE I KNOW — OR THE ONE WHO HOLDS THE TOKEN.

YES, I MUST FIND THAT BOY.

IN A LUMBERING CITY BUS...
CARLOS AND HIS MOTHER SIT IN
THE BACK ROW. AS HIS MOTHER DOZES,
CARLOS REACHES INTO HIS POCKET
AND PULLS THE TOKEN OUT, CURLING
HIS FINGERS OVER IT.

O'Leary's

PHNOM PENH
CAMBODIAN CUIS.

STARTLED BY THE SUDDEN LIGHT, CARLOS
SHOVES THE TOKEN BACK INTO HIS POCKET.
IT BECOMES DARK AGAIN.

YAWN!
MUST BE
TIRED.

CARLOS SLEEPS.

UNSEEN BY THE BOY...

THE TOKEN?

SNATCHED AWAY! BY A WRETCHED BOY! BUT MY PIGEONS FOLLOWED HIM HOME SO **I** KNOW WHERE HE LIVES.

THIS IS MY BEST CHANCE EVER!

I ALMOST HAD IT! ALMOST!

WHAT DO YOU MEAN?

I'M GOING TO GET THAT TOKEN FROM THE BOY.

WHAT CAN I DO?

THIS TIME IT'S ESTELLA WHOM I NEED.

I DON'T CARE WHAT YOU CALL HER!

BUT SARAH HAS NEVER MET YOU AND, BESIDES, SHE HAS SCHOOL. CAN'T I BE THE ONE WHO—

HER NAME IS **SARAH**!

MR. BITNER, WE HAVE AN UNDERSTANDING.

THE NAME IS STUBBS!

WELL THEN, "STUBBS"— THE SITUATION IS DELICATE. I CAN'T RISK ALARMING THE BOY. THERE'S NO LIKELIHOOD THE GIRL WILL DO THAT.

AND SHE'LL BE IN NO DANGER.

BUT...

43

RECUERDA QUE MAÑANA VOY A JERSEY PARA VER A TÍA NINA QUE ESTÁ ENFERMA. REGRESARÉ EL MIÉRCOLES.

QUISIERA IR CONTIGO. ESTA CIUDAD ES SUCIA Y ME ABURRE.

"NOW REMEMBER, TOMORROW I'M GOING TO JERSEY TO SEE SICK AUNT NINA. BE BACK WEDNESDAY."

"WISH I COULD GO. THIS CITY'S JUST DIRT AND DULLNESS."

LA MAMÁ DE TOM ESPERA QUE VAYAS A QUEDARTE CON ELLOS. TE LLAMARÉ ALLÍ POR LA NOCHE. ¿TIENES DINERO PARA EL AUTOBÚS?

"TOM'S MOTHER IS EXPECTING YOU TO STAY WITH THEM. I'LL CALL YOU THERE TOMORROW NIGHT. YOU HAVE BUS MONEY?"

TENGO UNA FICHA. ¿HAS VISTO ESA REVISTA CON UN PLANEADOR DE MANOS?

FIJÁTE QUE NO.

"A TOKEN. HAVE YOU SEEN THAT MAGAZINE WITH THE HANG GLIDER IN IT?"

"AFRAID NOT."

45

UNDERTON LIVES IN A FORTY-STORY BUILDING AT THE BOTTOM OF THE CITY.

THAT NIGHT THE BLIND MAN CANNOT SLEEP. HE PROWLS THE BUILDING, WANDERING THROUGH EMPTY ROOMS AND DESERTED FLOORS. EVERYWHERE HE GOES, SKOTOS FOLLOWS. FROM TIME TO TIME UNDERTON STOPS AND FACES THE OUTER GLASS WALLS. BEYOND THEM, HE KNOWS, IS THE CITY. THOUSANDS UPON THOUSANDS OF BUILDINGS WITH BRIGHT WINDOWS, LIGHTS TO OUTSHINE THE STARS. UNDERTON SEES NONE OF IT. BUT IN HIS MIND'S EYE HE SEES WHERE CARLOS LIVES. AND SEEING WHERE CARLOS LIVES, HE SEES THE TOKEN.

CLOSE, SO VERY CLOSE.
THE THOUGHT MAKES HIM CLENCH HIS FISTS IN RAGE. HE REMEMBERS ASTEREL. GRIEF GRIPS HIM, RECALLING HOW HE BECAME BLIND.
OH, FOR THE JOYS OF SIGHT!
THE SIGHT OF BLINKING, SHINING SIGNS FOR WHICH ARGON CREATES LAVENDER. ARGON AND MERCURY, MIXED, BRILLIANT BLUE, AND NEON FOR BRIGHT RED-ORANGE. PINK FROM HELIUM, AND FROM KRYPTON, A WHITISH PINK. BEST OF ALL, XENON! FOR A LOW, SILVERY, PURPLE GLOW.
THIS TIME, THE TOKEN WILL BE MINE.
AT LAST I WILL SEE AGAIN!

OUTSIDE THE STORE...

CANDY EMPORIUM
SWEETS TO SWEETEN SPIRITS
WELCOME! WE'RE ALWAYS OPEN!

I WONDER WHAT THIS IS ABOUT.

WHO IS THAT GIRL?

WHY AM I TREMBLING?

KIND OF YOU TO COME, MISS STUBBS.

MY FATHER ASKED ME TO.

WELL, THEN, LET US GO.

WHERE ARE WE GOING?

I WANT TO KNOW.

THIS GIRL IS TOUGHER THAN THEO.

I REQUIRE YOUR HELP IN GETTING BACK SOMETHING I LOST.

WHAT IS IT?

A TRANSIT TOKEN.

MR. UNDERTON, THERE ARE THOUSANDS, **MILLIONS** OF TOKENS!

I COULD GET YOU ONE IN MINUTES!

53

55

THE MOMENT SARAH EMERGES FROM SCHOOL, ASTEREL - WHO HAS WAITED ALL DAY FOR HER TO APPEAR - WATCHES INTENTLY. THEN CARLOS COMES OUT OF THE BUILDING. ASTEREL GIVES A START.

THE BOY WITH THE TOKEN!

BUT THE GIRL MOVES AWAY IN ONE DIRECTION, THE BOY IN ANOTHER. ONCE AGAIN ASTEREL IS TORN OVER WHOM TO FOLLOW.

CONSOLING HERSELF WITH THE KNOWLEDGE THAT SHE KNOWS WHERE THE GIRL LIVES, ASTEREL FALLS IN BEHIND THE BOY.

YOU GONNA TELL ME ABOUT THAT GIRL?

SAID HER NAME WAS SARAH.

OH, YEAH, SARAH STUBBS. WHAT DID SHE WANT?

CARLOS BEGINS BY EXPLAINING HOW HE GOT THE TOKEN AND FINISHES WITH SARAH'S ACCUSATION THAT HE STOLE IT.

THAT TRUE? YOU REALLY GOT IT FROM A BIRD?

HONEST! AND IT'S THE SAME AS ANY I EVER SAW.

LET'S SEE IT.

LEFT IT HOME.

HOW'D THAT GIRL KNOW ABOUT IT?

SAID SOME FRIEND OF HERS — A BLIND GUY — TOLD HER.

IF HE WAS BLIND, HOW'D HE KNOW?

DOESN'T MAKE SENSE, DOES IT? AND SHE EVEN SAID SHE'D GIVE ME MONEY FOR IT.

YOU GOING TO HAND IT OVER?

I DON'T KNOW.

UPSET, SARAH REPLACES THE LITTLE BOOK ON THE SHELF, THEN GOES UPSTAIRS. SHE TAKES THE PHOTO OF THE WOMAN SHE THOUGHT WAS HER MOTHER.

SARAH STARTS HER HOMEWORK, THE PHOTO BEFORE HER. FROM TIME TO TIME SHE GAZES AT IT. "IS THIS REALLY MY MOTHER?" SHE KEEPS ASKING HERSELF.

ON TOM'S ROOF...

66

73

75

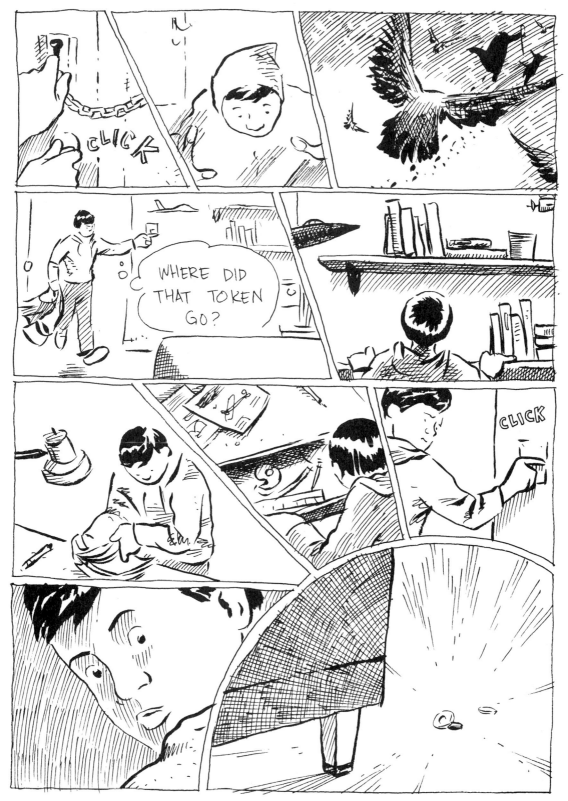

NOW CARLOS REMEMBERS THE BUS RIDE HOME FROM THE FAMILY PARTY. HADN'T HE HELD THE TOKEN THEN, AND HADN'T THINGS BECOME BRIGHT? THEY HAD! AND FINDING THE MAGAZINE! IT HAD BEEN WHILE HOLDING THE TOKEN THAT HE SAW **THROUGH** THE COUCH!

4TH CHAPTER

MOMENTS LATER...

BB-RING
RIIING

CARLOS!

¡HOLA, MAMÁ!

ACABA DE LLAMAR LA CASA DE TOM. ¿POR QUÉ NO TE QUEDASTE CON ELLOS?

OLVIDÉ.

ES MUY TARDE PARA IR AHORITA. PERO LLAMA LA MAMÁ DE TOM Y PROMETELE QUE VAS A QUEDARTE CON ELLOS MAÑANA.

"HI, MOM!"

"I JUST CALLED TOM'S. WHY DIDN'T YOU STAY WITH THEM?"

"I FORGOT."

"IT'S TOO LATE TO GO NOW. BUT CALL TOM'S MOTHER AND PROMISE YOU'LL STAY TOMORROW."

LO HARÉ. ¿COME SE SIENTE TÍA NINA?

MEJOR. ¿SABES QUÉ?

MAÑANA TENGO UNA ENTREVISTA AQUÍ PARA UN TRABAJO.

¡FANTÁSTICO! ¡OJALÁ QUE LO GANES!

"I WILL. HOW'S AUNT NINA?"

"FEELING BETTER. GUESS WHAT?"

"I HAVE A JOB INTERVIEW HERE TOMORROW."

"GREAT! HOPE YOU GET IT!"

BUENO, AMOR. ¿VAS A ESTAR BIEN? SÍ.

TE LLAMARÉ A CASA DE TOM. ADIOS.

"ALL RIGHT, LOVE. YOU GOING TO BE OKAY?" "YEAH."

"I'LL PHONE YOU TOMORROW AT TOM'S." "BYE."

BBRING

HELLO?

MAY I SPEAK TO CARLOS JUAREZ, PLEASE?

SPEAKING.

THIS IS SARAH STUBBS, THE ONE WHO ASKED YOU ABOUT THAT TOKEN. I NEED TO TALK TO YOU ABOUT IT.

WHAT FOR?

81

MR. STUBBS, HAVING RUN AWAY FROM SARAH, REACHES THE LOWER END OF THE CITY.

THIS CAN'T GO ON.

HAVE TO SEE HIM.

CLANG CLANG

I MUST COME TO SOME UNDERSTANDING WITH UNDERTON.

WHAT'S HAPPENED?

I WAITED FOR MY OPPORTUNITY TO GET THE TOKEN FROM THAT BOY ALL DAY.

AND?

84

85

86

87

89

THIS SARAH IS OKAY.

COOL. I'M PUTTING OUR PHONE NEXT TO MY BED. IF YOU NEED ANYTHING, ANYTIME, CALL.

OKAY.

I MEAN IT. ANYTIME.

ALL RIGHT. TELL ME WHAT'S HAPPENING.

SARAH TELLS CARLOS WHAT SHE KNOWS ABOUT UNDERTON.

I WISH I KNEW WHY MY FATHER HAS BEEN GIVING HIM MONEY.

THEN SHE TELLS HIM ABOUT HER DISCOVERIES THAT DAY CONCERNING HER MOTHER'S PICTURE.

YOU MEAN, YOU'VE NEVER SEEN YOUR MOTHER?

NEVER.

WELL, I HARDLY EVER SEE MY FATHER.

I TRIED TO TALK TO MY FATHER. HE JUST RAN OFF. I COULDN'T JUST SIT HOME. SO I DECIDED TO COME OVER.

CARLOS, HOW **DID** YOU GET THE TOKEN?

93

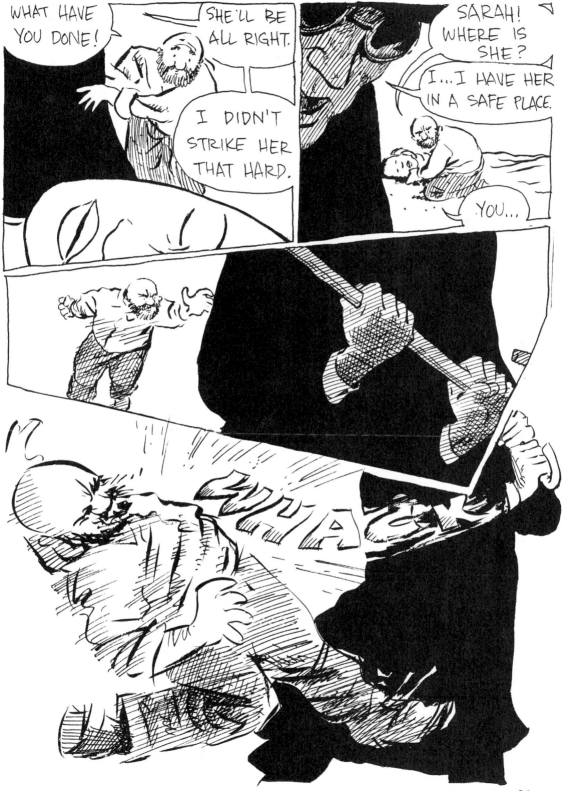

101

105

SPONGY AND SHRILL. SHADOW AND SMOKE. PEOPLE SEE THEM ALL THE TIME WITHOUT REALIZING.

WHAT'S UNDERTON HAVE TO DO WITH THEM?

ESTELLA HEARS THE TRUTH ABOUT UNDERTON.

MY FATHER HAS BEEN PAYING HIM MONEY FOR YEARS.

IN RETURN HE PROMISES TO PROTECT YOUR FATHER FROM ME.

WHY?

SARAH LEARNS HOW ASTEREL AND THEO MET, ABOUT THEIR LOVE, MARRIAGE, AND CHILD.

MAYBE MY FATHER DIDN'T KNOW WHERE YOU WERE.

HE CAME TO ME TONIGHT.

BUT WHEN YOU HAD THE TOKEN, COULDN'T YOU SEE ME?

I HAVE THE POWER TO SEE WHO HAS THE TOKEN. TO SEE ANYONE ELSE, I MUST KNOW **EXACTLY** WHAT THEY LOOK LIKE. YOUR FATHER TOOK ON A DISGUISE TO PREVENT MY SEEING HIM.

AS FOR YOU, I LOOKED FOR YOU EVERYWHERE I WENT. BUT THE TWO-DAY-OLD BABY I KNEW NO LONGER EXISTS, DOES SHE?

UNDERTON TOOK CARE NEVER TO COME HERE. THIS MORNING HE DID, AND WHEN I FOLLOWED HIM I SAW YOU FOR THE FIRST TIME.

BUT WE DON'T HAVE TO JUST SIT HERE, DO WE? COULDN'T WE AT LEAST **TRY** LOOKING FOR MY FATHER?

UNDERTON IS COUNTING ON YOU IN YOUR DISTRESS TO DO SOMETHING FOOLISH. BESIDES, ESTELLA, IN THIS CITY IT'S POSSIBLE TO HIDE THINGS — AND PEOPLE — FOREVER. I HAVE NO IDEA WHERE TO BEGIN.

I NEED SOME SLEEP.

GRASP IT.

WHY?

JUST THINK OF WHAT YOU NEED.

SLEEP?

YOU NEED **POWER**. POWER — ENERGY.

HEY — I FEEL GREAT AGAIN. NO LONGER TIRED.

MY TURN.

WHAT ABOUT GOING TO THE KURBS, SHOWING THEM THAT WE'VE GOT THE TOKEN BUT, YOU KNOW, ASKING FOR AN EXTENSION.

RIGHT. IF THEY KNEW WE HAD IT, MAYBE THEY WOULD UNDERSTAND.

I TOLD YOU: STAY AS FAR AWAY FROM THEM AS POSSIBLE. THEY'RE VERY DANGEROUS.

IF THERE ARE ANY KURBS ABOUT! I HAVE THE TOKEN!
I WANT TO GO TO THE CHIEF KURB!
SKREEEEEL SKREEEEEEEL
SKRE EEEEEEEL
ESTELLA! YOU MUSTN'T!
SKREEEE
THE KURBS ARE DANGEROUS!
AFTER TWENTY MINUTES OF HARD RUNNING THROUGH EMPTY, SNOWY STREETS...
FOLLOW THAT KURB!

119

SARAH STEPS FORWARD. THE SHRIEKS, CRIES, AND SQUEALS OF THE KURBS GROW LOUDER, IN WAVE UPON WAVE OF DEAFENING NOISE. THEN, GRADUALLY, THE NOISE BEGINS TO SUBSIDE UNTIL IT BECOMES A HUM, A MURMUR, THEN— SILENCE.

HOW DARE YOU COME
HERE, CHILD!
THIS PLACE IS FORBIDDEN TO PEOPLE.
YOU TEST OUR ANGER,
AND WE TELL YOU, CHILD, THAT NEVER IN
ALL THE YEARS HAVE WE EXTENDED THE
DEADLINE. NOT BY A DAY. NOT AN HOUR.
NOT ONE SECOND. NEVER.
THE LAND YOU PEOPLE LIVE ON BELONGS TO
US, THE KURBS. IT HAS ONLY BEEN LOANED
TO YOU. IF YOU FAIL TO FULFILL
THE RITUAL CYCLE OF ACKNOWLEDGMENT,
WE WILL TAKE OUR ISLAND BACK. O CHILD,
YOU WHO HAVE THE TOKEN, LISTEN!

THE RITUAL INSISTS THE TOKEN SHALL BE IN ITS REQUIRED PLACE OF SAFEKEEPING BY THE TWENTY-FIRST DAY OF DECEMBER, AT THE STROKE OF NOON, OR YOU PEOPLE SHALL SUFFER THE CONSEQUENCES! THE DEADLINE IS TODAY! BE WARNED!

WHAT'S HAPPENING?

I THINK THEY'RE SENDING US AWAY.

GUESS WE BETTER GO.

TWENTY MINUTES OF WALKING BRINGS THEM TO A MASSIVE DOOR. AS THEY APPROACH, THE DOOR OPENS AND THEY PASS THROUGH. THEY ARE BACK IN THE ABANDONED EIGHTEENTH STREET SUBWAY STATION.

127

STAY WHERE YOU ARE! THERE'S NO WAY OFF THIS TRAIN!

WE'RE GOING TOO FAST. WE CAN'T GET OFF.

I WANT THAT TOKEN NOW!

HE'S COMING!

LET'S GET TO THE FRONT END! MAYBE HE CAN'T FOLLOW US.

THE TRAIN IS FIVE CARS LONG. SARAH AND CARLOS HAVE TO OPEN AND CLOSE THE DOORS OF EACH CAR BEFORE REACHING THE NEXT. BY THE TIME THEY GET TO THE FRONT CAR, THEY HAVE PASSED STILL ANOTHER STATION.

AT THE FINAL CAR THEY LOOK BACK.

HE'S STILL COMING!

WHAT'S THIS DOOR? THE DRIVER'S BOX! MAYBE WE CAN STOP THE TRAIN AT THE NEXT STATION.

OH OH! HE'S IN THE NEXT CAR!

CARLOS, WHICH LEVER?

I DON'T KNOW.

ONE OF THESE MUST BE A THROTTLE.

THE OTHER SHOULD BE THE BRAKE.

TRY TO KEEP HIM OUT! I'LL TRY TO STOP US.

130

133

136

AT TOM'S APARTMENT...
UNDERTON'S BEGINNING TO WALK. I THINK HIS PIGEONS ARE LEADING HIM. CARLOS!

WHAT?

I THINK HE'S COMING THIS WAY.

WOULD SOMEONE PLEASE TELL ME WHAT'S GOING ON?

IT'S THAT GUY I TOLD YOU ABOUT—UNDERTON. HE'S HOLDING SARAH'S FATHER HOSTAGE SOMEWHERE UNTIL HE GETS THE TOKEN. ONLY WE'VE GOT IT NOW, SO HE'S AFTER US.

THE THING IS, WE HAVE TO FIND MY FATHER BEFORE NOON.

WHAT HAPPENS THEN?

TOO COMPLICATED TO TELL YOU NOW. WE JUST HAVE TO, THAT'S ALL.

YOU HAVE THAT TOKEN WITH YOU?

WHERE'S THAT GUY NOW?

LOOKS ORDINARY TO ME.

THAT'S HOW SHE WAS ABLE TO CALL YOU.

THIS?

JUST A COUPLE OF BLOCKS AWAY.

THAT TOKEN TELL YOU?

IT'S GOT POWER LIKE THAT.

HOW DOES HE TRACK YOU?

I'M NOT SURE.

WELL, HE CAN'T GET IN HERE. MY DAD FIXED IT GOOD.

WHAT'S HAPPENING?

HE'S RIGHT AT THE CORNER.

THUMP THUMP

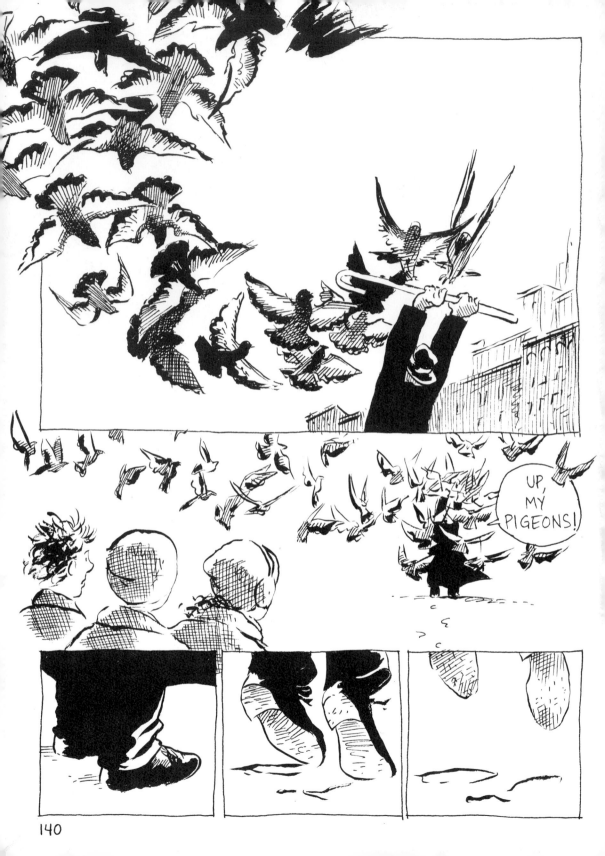

143

145

155

167

BY THE TIME THE BOAT REACHES THE DOCK, A STORM HAS BEGUN, A DRIVING, SLEETING STORM THAT COVERS EVERY SURFACE OF THE BOAT WITH A CRUST OF SLIPPERY ICE.

THE THREE BARELY WAIT FOR THE GANG-PLANK TO BE LET DOWN BEFORE THEY RUSH OFF INTO THE STREET.

THE WEATHER WORSENS.
WHIRLING SNOW MAKES IT ALL
BUT IMPOSSIBLE TO SEE. VICIOUS
WINDS CAREEN UP AND DOWN THE
STREETS, BUFFETING ALL WHO
DARE TO BRAVE THEM. SO DARK IS
IT THAT STREET LAMPS HAVE
COME ON. LAMPPOSTS RATTLE.
HYDRANTS FREEZE. PEOPLE
WALK HUNCHED OVER, HOLDING
DOWN COATS, TRYING TO INSULATE
THEMSELVES FROM THE CUTTING
EDGES OF THE WIND.

TRAFFIC IS AT A CRAWL. THE
INCESSANT GRINDING OF FROZEN
AUTO ENGINES FILLS THE AIR
WITH GROANS THAT SET TEETH
ON EDGE.

STUBBS, SARAH, AND CARLOS STRUGGLE DOWN INTO THE NEAREST SUBWAY. THEY WAIT FOR A TRAIN. IT IS TOO COLD FOR TALK. BETWEEN THE TRACKS POOLS OF WATER TURN TO ICE.

IN THE SUBWAY RIDERS ARE QUIETER THAN NORMAL, BUT THEY MUTTER ABOUT THE LACK OF HEAT. EVERY BREATH IS CLOUDED WITH COLD. HANDS ARE WRUNG. FEET TAP.

MINUTE BY MINUTE THE COLD DEEPENS.

THE CITY IS FREEZING.

179

180

183

THE LAST CHAPTER

¿ADIVINA QUE PASÓ?

NO PUEDO.

THAT NIGHT... CARLOS, AS HE HAD PROMISED HIS MOTHER, IS AT TOM'S APARTMENT. HE AND TOM HAVE ALREADY DECIDED NOT TO TELL THE ADULTS WHAT HAPPENED, BECAUSE THEY ARE CERTAIN NO GROWN-UP WOULD BELIEVE IT.

AFTER DINNER, CARLOS'S MOTHER CALLS.

"GUESS WHAT'S HAPPENED?"

"CAN'T."

ME OFRECIERON EL TRABAJO AQUÍ.

¿EN EL CAMPO?

EXACTAMENTE LO QUE QUIERES.

BUENO, MAMÁ, NO ESTOY MUY SEGURO QUE QUIERO IR.

¡CARLOS! ¿QUE HA PASADO CONTIGO?

ESTAN PASANDO COSAS INTERESANTES.

"I GOT A JOB OFFER OUT HERE."

"IN THE COUNTRY?"

"JUST WHAT YOU WANTED."

"YEAH, WELL, MA, I'M NOT SO SURE I WANT TO GO."

"CARLOS! WHAT'S COME OVER YOU?"

"THERE'S SOME INTERESTING STUFF GOING ON...."

SARAH GAVE THAT SPECIAL TOKEN TO THE DOG BY MISTAKE, RIGHT? BEFORE YOU GOT HERE LAST NIGHT. ISN'T THAT WHAT YOU SAID?

RIGHT. WE'RE PRETTY LUCKY UNDERTON DIDN'T GET IT.

OKAY, THEN HOW COME, IF SHE **DIDN'T** HAVE THE TOKEN, SHE WAS ABLE TO DO ALL THAT STUFF?

YOU KNOW, LIKE SEEING THINGS IN HER HEAD, GIVING POWER TO THE PLANE? ALL THAT STUFF. THAT'S WHAT I DON'T UNDERSTAND. DO YOU KNOW WHAT I'M SAYING?

YOU'RE RIGHT.

AFTER SARAH GAVE THE TOKEN TO SKOTOS, I COULDN'T DO ANYTHING WITH THE TOKEN.

BUT SHE COULD.

WELL?

I'M NOT SURE. LET'S ASK HER AT SCHOOL TOMORROW.

THE NEXT WEEKEND, IN ASTEREL'S CAVE...

WHAT SHALL I BE NEXT YEAR? DOGCATCHER? FIREFIGHTER? ICE-CREAM VENDOR?

MA?

HOW **DID** I DO ALL THAT STUFF?

BECAUSE YOU ARE MY DAUGHTER, ESTELLA, AND ALL MY POWERS ARE YOUR POWERS.

THEY ARE?

REMEMBER, IN YOUR FATHER'S HOUSE, JUST BEFORE YOU AND CARLOS RAN OFF, I PRESSED THE TOKEN TO YOUR FOREHEAD?

THAT IS EXACTLY WHAT I HAD TO DO RIGHT AFTER YOU WERE BORN, THE REASON I HAD HELD ONTO THE TOKEN. ONCE I ANOINTED YOU, I GAVE YOU ALL MY POWERS BECAUSE, WELL, AFTER ALL, YOU ARE MY DAUGHTER.

NOW YOU KNOW HOW I CAME TO BE THE SEARCHER OF THE TOKEN. IT WAS MY MOTHER BEFORE ME, AS IT WAS HER MOTHER BEFORE HER, WHO DID THE SAME. OH, WE COME FROM AN ANCIENT PEOPLE, ESTELLA. SO SOMEDAY, WHAT I DO, YOU TOO SHALL DO.

ME? AM I REALLY TO BE LIKE YOU?

OH, YES, THE SAME. BUT YOURSELF, TOO.

DO I GET TO CHOOSE WHAT I WANT TO BE EACH AND EVERY YEAR?

YES.

BUT NOT FOR A WHILE, RIGHT?

NOT FOR A WHILE.